The Email Marketing Playbook
New Strategies to get your Emails Noticed

Author: Adella Pasos

Are you interested in learning how email marketing can improve your business and profits? Tired of getting nowhere fast? Either if you want to make some extra cash on the side working a few hours per week or building a real business that will provide you with a full time income, so you can quit your job and work from wherever you want.

The email marketing playbook is a strategic guide that explains how to get started in email marketing, how to get people on your list and the best types of email tactics to use so you can start making money online today and grow your business. In this book you will learn how to work with an email blast provider, grow a list and build high quality email marketing campaigns, just like "the Big Guys Do".

If you want to learn everything you'll ever need to know about email marketing, this is the book for you!

The Email Marketing Playbook
New Strategies to get your Emails Noticed

Published by Adella Pasos

Copyright © 2020 www.adellapasos.com

All rights reserved. No part of this book, including interior design, cover design, and icons may be reproduced or transmitted in any form, by any means (electronic, photocopying, recording or otherwise) without the prior written permission of the author, except for the inclusion of brief quotations in a review.

Table of Contents

Introduction: About This Book

Chapter 1: Email Marketing Basics

This chapter discusses how effective email marketing will convert prospects into customers and turns buyers into loyal fans. Also included is best practice samples for email marketing.

Chapter 2: Choosing an Email Provider

Email marketing is a profitable business, but which platform is right for you? Find out which email marketing software is right for you before your signup.

Chapter 3: How to Generate Subscribers

This chapter shares with you the most effective ways to get subscribers on your email list and turn them into sales.

Chapter 4: Creating Your First Campaign

Learn how to create stunning email campaigns in minutes. This beginner's guide will ensure you get it right the first time.

Chapter 5: Powerful Headlines That Get People to Open Emails

This chapter includes a list of catchy subject lines that get people to open immediately and read what you have to say.

Table of Contents Continued...

Chapter 6: What to Say in Emails In Order to Sell

This chapter provides a list of email templates that give you exactly what to say in order to persuade someone to buy your products or services.

Chapter 7: How to Interpret Data & Email Results

To help you figure out what you should be measuring, this chapter covers all the important KPI's you should be looking at on your reports and how to improve the numbers.

Chapter 8: Ways to Automate the Email Marketing Process

Email automation is the most effective way to engage in email marketing because it enables you to send out messages to your customers at designated times. Make money in your sleep.

Chapter 9: Email Marketing Resources

This chapter includes a list of impressive email marketing template links for various niches. So you can design beautiful campaigns to effectively communicate with your audience and share your message.

Appendix: Frequently Asked Questions

This is a great spot to check out the most common questions people have other ways to make money and benefits of email marketing.

Introduction: About This E-Book

Hello! and thanks for downloading this awesome book. Throughout the course of this book you will learn how to create, promote and profit from email marketing. I wrote this book for you to truly see that your business can succeed with a great email marketing strategy.

The strategies that I've listed in the book will explain how you can get paid from using email marketing, as well as where and how to get started. Entrepreneurs, start-ups, and even large fortune 500 companies are using the same strategies to gain millions of dollars. So, where's your piece of the pie? Who doesn't love a fast track to success?

Who am I?

I am an International Business Coach and Marketing Strategist who has shared my passion for growing brands from the ground up. I've worked with startups, small businesses, global corporations and entertainment talent that recognize the value of marketing. I give my clients the ability to sell more by preparing them with the right strategies in social media, mobile, merchandising, and events. Providing simple solutions to complex challenges, I've placed all that I know into these books.

Now, it's time for you to apply the knowledge, and get out there and put your game face on!

Cheers to your success,

Adella Pasos

Chapter 1: Email Marketing Basics

Why Content Marketing?

Email marketing is super important for building relationships with prospects, leads, current customers and even past customers because it gives you a chance to speak directly to them, in their inbox, at a time that is convenient for them. Since they've already given you permission to send them more information on items they may be interested in buying. Email marketing also allows you to send them your sales on products or services, specials and promotional items.

How Event Marketing Helps

- Save valuable marketing budget dollars
- Increase brand recognition
- Connect with your target market Increase your credibility
- Educate your current clients
- Attract new opportunities
- Create new streams of income
- Expand your network
- Unlimited opportunity to connect
- Easily generate sales without a large budget
- Allows you to get started quickly

What are the Benefits of Email Marketing?

The main advantages of email marketing vs traditional marketing are:

- Emails are delivered extremely fast when compared to mail.
- Emails can be sent 24 hours a day, 365 days a year.
- Emails can be sent and received from any computer, anywhere in the world, that has an Internet connection.
- Email is one of the most cheapest forms of marketing.

How Do I Start?

Step 1: Establish Your Email Strategy

The first step is deciding on the main goal of your email. It can be multiple goals for example: to collect leads, to sell, to help decision makers remember you, to collect feedback from customers, etc. A good place to start is to define at least 3-5 specific goals.

Step 2: Start Developing the Content

The next step is to 'brand' your content. All email content needs to be professionally designed so that it is memorable and specific to meet your goals. I prefer to use [99designs](), they are the most reliable for marketing design work.

Step 3: Decide on the type of campaign you want to send

After you've got your content designed, you'll need to decide on the type of campaign you want to launch. A good place to start is to work backwards from your goal. If your goal is to generate a sale, you'll need to decide on how many emails need to be sent and what kind (one time offer, sales promo, general follow up, tips and tricks, etc).

Step 4: Start building your list

After you've decided on the type of campaign you want to run, it's time to start building your list. This means participating in marketing activities that will prompt people to join. Remember, most people only join for the following reasons: to receive promotions and discounts, to receive exclusive content or VIP offers, or to show continued support for a company / brand and receive your updates.

Step 5: Measure your results

There are many methods to promote your content and persuading people to sign up. Whether you choose from organic methods or paid methods to drive traffic, always measure your results from each traffic source. This way, you can cut the clutter and invest time and resources only in methods that are driving the highest results.

Most email providers come equipped with an analytics dashboard. This will tell you where you are and where you can improve. Each email sent is chance to better your business and refine your sales strategy.

How Do I Get Paid?

Are you an aspiring startup entrepreneur or an established business owner? Earning money with email marketing by promoting other people's (or company's) products or promoting your own products and/or services. Many people starting out choose to use an inbound lead generation strategy that consist of creating videos, writing blog posts and articles, webinars, email blasts, and promoting through social media and live events.

These options will drive traffic to your email list, where you can send the customers what you are selling. Make sure you pick a product or service that you feel comfortable selling. Your only job is to promote the list and send them what they are expecting to receive.

Here's a list of ways to make money from email:

- Sell products on your Thank You page after they first opt-in
- Send your audience a list of your daily, weekly or monthly promos
- Segment your list and send your audience personalized suggestions
- After a buyer makes a purchase, send them an email up-selling another product or service.
- Add a link to buy your products or services at the end of your emails
- Giveaway a free guide via email and add links to buy your products and services in it
- Add affiliate links to your emails and promote partner programs
- Sell ads in your newsletter to brands

Email Marketing Best Practices

Here is a list of key things to remember that will help you along the way.

1) Build Your Own List

Resist the temptation of buying a list. Sending unexpected or what could seem to be spam email to people who don't know about you or have not accepted to be on your email list will likely end up in the spam folder and your email address will end up on a blacklist.

If you don't have the time or money to invest in traffic to build your own list, the next best thing is to pay for an email sponsorship or email promotion with a trusted network who has spent time nurturing and growing their list. Before you pay, make sure you discuss the targeting options and promotional advertisement sizes to get the best bang for your buck. You can easily build your own list by promoting your email sign-up on your website, blog, landing pages, videos, and any other content marketing you create.

2) Don't forget to insert a Call to Action (CTA) and close the sale

It's not enough to put a bunch of persuasive information in your emails, but not tell them where they can buy it or ask the customer to buy. Your call to action is one of the most important pieces of content in your email.

After you have a subscriber, your next goal is to get your subscribers to click on your content and buy whatever you are selling / promoting. Imagine it to be a regular conversation between you and a friend. What would you say to get your friend to buy?

3) Don't Reinvent the Wheel

If you are not fluent in coding html or graphic design, you have **OPTIONS!** Whether you need to use a template or hire a developer or designer, the email's overall look should align with your brand. Make sure the fonts, colors, styling look good and match what's on your website, business cards etc. Also don't over complicate the email, make it look simple. Again, the most important thing is to get the customer to click where you need them to go to buy the product or service. I use **Canva** or create custom email designs or hire a professional designer through **99designs.**

4) Don't Go So Hard

Sometimes we have a tendency to send too many emails over and over because we are anxious to get people to buy. You never want your emails to seem spammy or too promotional. Most people signed up to your list because they are interested in specific information or content.

Before asking your subscribers to purchase anything or sign up for a service, **offer them something of value first**. Give good information or tips, tell them about what you have going on and outline why your product may be a good fit for them. You can even send an email asking them to fill out a form for a time to discuss if they have additional questions or give them a link to the FAQ section of your website.

Always include a CTA (call to action) for those who are ready to buy and need the product immediately. For those who don't, continue to add value, suggestions can come in the form of how-to-material, a demo video or just a simple article that answers some of the frequently asked questions about the product or service you are trying to sell.

5) Pay Attention to Engagement Numbers

If people are opening your emails, but not clicking through to your intended destination (website, sale page, product page). Then you have a problem. You'll need to redefine what kind of content goes in the email blast.

Maybe you are sending content the person didn't expect, maybe the content isn't useful to them, or maybe they were only interested in one product / service only and are waiting for sale. You can easily find out by sending out a survey asking each person from the list to tell you what they are interested in seeing more of.

Here's a list of things you can send to your email subscribers:

Welcome Email - with a Coupon Discount Offer $ off or % off , free trial offers

Best Sellers List - Showing the top purchased or most popular products

A Survey Email - Asking their opinion on products / or what they want

Please Review Us Email - Ask them for a Product Review in exchange for a discount on their next purchase or a gift card

An Solutions Video Email - Showing How Your Product / Services Work

An Demo Request Email - Asking them to book an appointment or sign up for product demo

Event Invitation - Asking them to attend an online webinar to learn more or attend a meet and greet

Case Study Email - Showing them other companies / people who love or have had success with your product or service / testimonials

Content Digest Email - Promote your blog post, articles, press, thought leadership, podcasts, ebooks, infographics

Opinion RoundUp - Collect their opinions and then send the results back to them next week on the poll and include the popular vote and a link to buy

Quiz - Using quizzes via email will help generate leads and learn who is interested in actually buying. Quizzes can work for any industry to help personalize your website and sell products without a huge up-front investment.

VIP Club - Send your subscribers a special invite to get special VIP deals, discounts offers or invite them to a closed facebook group. This will make them look for your emails faster and increase the open rates.

Pre-Order - Allow your subscribers to get first dibs on your new product or service you are releasing. Take pre-orders and get sales immediately.

Deal of the Day - Email stating your one day only promotions

REMINDER: You need to be able to convince the customer that they need the product, that it is a priority to buy, that it is widely accepted, that there is little to no risk involved in buying, there is much value and buying helps them complete their goals. Most customers will go through the general thought process of *"what's my problem?", "how do I fix my problem?"* and *"are you the right solution for my problem?"* Make sure your emails can always answer those questions.

Chapter 2: Choosing an Email Marketing Provider

Email software will likely be the primary means by which you deliver engaging content, deals, personalized messages, and expanding your list of customers. Email marketing services and tools allow you to get the highest ROI possible by automating your workflows, tracking opens, clicks, and replies, and gaining you more mailing list subscribers. But sometimes, it can be hard to know which service is the best.

Here's a list of the top providers and their benefits:

Constant Contact: Best for Small Business. <u>Free Trial for 60 days.</u> Cost: $5-$45/mo

One tool, for all your marketing. That's the Constant Contact toolkit. Our customers get real results through marketing campaigns like email newsletters, surveys, events, Facebook promotions, online listings building tools, coupon tools and more.

AWeber: Best for Bloggers, Startups & Large Companies: <u>Free Trial for 30 Days.</u> Cost: $19-$149/mo.

Even the basic pricing includes unlimited contacts, unlimited emails, workflow automation, list segmentation, analytics, facebook promos, coupons, customer solutions, signup forms, integrations, free stock photos, 700+ templates and training resources. They also give you phone support to experts who help you grow. ***It's the best bang for your buck!***

When choosing a provider, you should ask yourself the following questions to help you come to a clear decision:

- What does my company want to achieve with email marketing?
- What are the costs and can we afford it?
- Do I understand how to get people to sign up for our email newsletters?
- Should I use a template or a custom design?
- Will I need help planning an email strategy?
- Do I want social elements added into my email marketing?
- Where will I get images for my email marketing?
- What level of customer support should my company expect?
- What type of reports will I get to measure the effectiveness of my campaigns?

Chapter 3: How To Generate Subscribers

The more email subscribers you have the more potential you have to make money. You want to build the biggest list you can possible and make sure the people are active, being nurtured and served the information they want.

These key points here are make sure you have a clean looking design, engaging content, a valuable offer and a call to action. Don't give away any of the content without getting an email address first. First, you need to lure them in, then capture the email, then send them the products / services promotion. **People are signing up to email lists for the following three reasons:**

1. To receive promotions and discounts
2. To receive exclusive content or VIP offers
3. To show continued support for an company or brand
4. To receive your updates

List of Ways to Get People On Your List

1. Add Opt-in Box on Your Home Page as a Popup upon entering your site

2. Add Opt-in Box in the Footer on Your Homepage with a discount coupon in exchange for their email address

3. Add Opt-in Box to Every Blog Page in the Right Column promoting a free ebook, consultation, product or offer

4. Add Opt-in Link to Your Email Signature

5. Add a link to a Landing Page which allows an email Opt-In from your Facebook, Twitter and IG Profile

6. Add Signup Button to your Facebook Page

7. Add / Pin a Signup Post to the Top of your Twitter Page

8. Promote a Sale of an item via SEM & Banner ads, send the traffic to an Opt-In email subscribe page

9. Buy an Email Sponsorship or Solo Ad that sends traffic to a Landing Page that allows opt-in to your list in exchange for something of value

10. Add a game or "spin to win" social contest to your website that engages visitors and captures emails.

11. Set Up an online webinar for those who are interested in learning more about your products / services and capturing email addresses.

12. Invite people to subscribe through your social networks, create a post sending them to a landing page or form to enter their email address

13. Invite your blog readers to subscribe and join a live event you are hosting

14. Advertise a product or service using SEM or Media Buying tactics and send all traffic to an opt-in landing page

15. Conduct a product / service giveaway and ask for email addresses to enter to win.

16. Offer a free video tutorial or how to use your product / service in exchange for an email address

17. Offer a Birthday or VIP Club - Give them something free in exchange for their email address

18. Ask your current customers to encourage friends to sign up to your list and give them a discount for every new person they get signed up.

19. Create Videos, upload to Youtube and Vimeo - include a link to your email signup page at the end of each video and in the description

20. Ask them to sign up at the end of check out on your website. Just because they are buying, doesn't mean they are on the list.

Chapter 4: Creating Your First Campaign

An email campaign is a coordinated set of email marketing messages delivered at intervals and designed to escalate a persuasive argument to purchase, subscribe, download, etc.

What are the first steps?

1. Identify the need for the email
2. Write down what the campaign will require
3. Choose an Email Design Template
4. Draft the email copy, find artwork or upload pics of your products
5. Add the copy and artwork to your template
6. Set up google tracking and add choose the list of recipients
7. Test your email first and make any edits required
8. Launch: Send Your Blast!

What are the best times to send emails?

Most data driven studies say between 8am-10 a.m. While late-morning send times were the most popular in general, the best time to send emails is at 10 a.m. because that's when people have time to look for their mail.

Another notable time is between 8 p.m. to midnight if you want to capture their attention. I bet you didn't expect that one. It looks like emails generally receive more opens and clicks later in the evening.

Chapter 5: Powerful Headlines That Get People to Open Emails

The subject line determines whether or not an email is opened and how the recipient will respond. If the Email has a blank subject line it will usually get deleted, lost or make the recipient annoyed. The subject line should be short and sweet. Most people stick to 50 characters or less. Those have higher open rates.

50 Sample Subject Lines

The most important thing about crafting these subject lines is you need to write them to sound like you are talking to someone or a friend. You'll need to spark curiosity, urgency, provide a cool story or reason for them to open, and personalize the message.

1. "Question about [goal]"
2. "[Mutual connection] recommended I get in touch"
3. "Our next steps"
4. "Do not open this email"
5. "X options to get started"
6. "Hi [name], [question]?"
7. "Did you get what you were looking for?"
8. "A [benefit] for [prospect's company]"
9. "X tips/ideas for [pain point]"
10. "You are not alone."
11. "Permission to close your file?"
12. "10 mins -- [date]?"
13. "We have [insert fact] in common ..."

14. [Prospect], I thought you might like these products ..

15. [Prospect], I thought you might like these blogs ... "

16. "Feeling [insert emotion]? Let me help"

17. "Uh-oh, your discount is expiring"

18. [URGENT] You've got ONE DAY to watch this..."

19. [WEEKEND ONLY] Get this NOW before it's gone..."

20. Mary, Earn double points today only"

21. This Week Only! 50% Off - Text to Win!

22. "Last Day To See What This Sale Is All About"

23. "Check out our new (ADD PRODUCTS HERE) [PICS]"

24. "Hottest Way to Do XYZ Right Now"

25. "These Pair nicely what your favorite shirt"

26. "Don't wear last year's styles."

27. "Your Butt Will Look Great in These Workout Pants"

28. "Age-defying beauty tricks"

29. "As worn on the Red Carpet this Week"

30. "Meet your new jeans"

31. "Get a head start on summer"

32. "New must-haves for your office"

33. "25% off your favorites"

34. "A little luxury at a great price"

35. "Get priority access."

36. "Feed your guests without breaking the bank"

37. "Get more kitchen space with these easy fixes"

38. "How to Survive Your Next Overnight Flight"

39. "Hey, forget something? Here's 20% off."

40. "Offering you my personal advice"

41. "Good News: The [PRODUCT NAME's] price dropped!"

42. "I didn't see your name in the comments!

43. "Vanilla or Chocolate?"

44. "Seriously, Who DOES This?"

45. "Are you free this Thursday at 12PM PST? [product demo]"

46. "Happy Holidays from [Company Name]"

47. FREE Delivery! Limited Time Only. All orders over $50.

48. Back in Stock! [Insert Product Name] Get Yours Today!

49. "You're missing out on points."

50. "Exclusive! Tonight only: A denim lover's dream"

Chapter 6: What to Say in Emails in Order to Sell

Selling is about your prospects, not about your company. A simple way to make that clear is by using the word **"you"** as much as possible. The key to selling via email is understanding the customer's problem, showing them how they are qualified to buy your product or service, convincing them to believe they need it and it will work for them, giving the assurance that there is a money back guarantee and that its prices for them to afford.

Position your product to the customer as a benefit to helping them achieve their goals.

Use **direct value statements** like " We assist our customers (list type of customers here) in the industry to _____. We do this by _____.

This answers the question in their mind *"what do you do or what do you sell?"* Normally, most people are interested in being wealthy, gaining extra income, look and feel better, be more healthy, be popular or liked amongst their friends / family, have security, achieve inner peace, have more free time, or have fun / be entertained.

To meet these needs, you'll need to create the right image and custom tailor your messaging so that it describes your product or service as "balanced, risk-free, specifically designed for XYZ, takes out the guesswork, no-nonsense, stable, as a huge return on investment, predictable, automatic, flexible, unique, reliable, responsive, sophisticated, quick setup, gives them a competitive advantage. This is what people want to hear.

First, build trust with familiarity. Show them that the product comes in a variety shapes or sizes, and that you have a wide selection. Detail in your message the ease of use, beautiful design, show and tell how other people are using and who is using it.

Second, having an enticing offer will give your recipients a good reason to respond and want to attain whatever you are giving them. Let them know how many you have available and that your price is lowest. Here's a list of words that make your offer sound enticing:

- Never Released Before
- The Latest
- One of a kind
- More for Less
- Why pay more?
- Blowout Sale!
- Become a machine
- Boost your by tonight
- Affordable
- Low-Cost
- Get everything for the price of one
- More value for money
- Save time on
- Free of Charge
- Here' a gift for you, simply for
- This is valued at $_____ but it's yours for FREE.
- Bonus!
- At no extra cost
- No additional charge
- If you act now, you also get
- Premium
- Only for a select few
- Instantly
- Just got easier

Third, Social proof. One of your biggest barriers to selling is risk. Many people are influenced by confidence. You can show even more confidence by telling them exactly when your product will sell out.

Showing video or written testimonials / review or having a statement of how many happy customers you've had can help increase sales and improve purchase rate. Here are a list of words that make people feel safe buying from you:

- Authentic
- Backed by Best Selling
- Cancel Anytime
- Endorsed by
- Guaranteed
- Lifetime Money Back
- No Risk
- Proven Results
- Success
- Tested
- Verified
- Accurate
- Certified
- Earned
- Unconditional
- No Obligation

Last, If you want to make your products or services sound exclusive and get people to subscribe or buy faster, use these words:

- Membership Discount
- Invite Only
- VIP members Only
- Ask for an Invitation
- First 50 Customers Offer
- Become an Insider
- Be one of the few
- Get it before everyone else
- Skip the Line
- Only available to subscribers
- Registration Almost Full
- Limited Time Offer
- While Supplies Last
- Sale Ending Today!
- Only 10 Available

Chapter 7: How to Interpret Data & Email Results

To help you figure what you should be measuring, here's a list of key performance indicators (KPIs) for email marketing. If you've been running various campaigns, with different content, subject line variations and goals how do you know whether they're successful or not? Pay attention to these numbers, they will truly help you optimize your campaigns depending on how high or low these numbers are.

Conversion - With every email you should be measuring how many people purchased vs how many emails were sent and to how many recipients.

Open rate - You should be measuring how many people open each message.

Click-through rate - Measure how many people click and what they are clicking (links vs buttons vs images vs videos).

Unsubscribe rate - Keep an eye on how many people are unsubscribing so that you don't come off as annoying.

Spam complaint rate - Monitor this so you can make changes to your campaign

Bounce rate - Monitor this so you can clean up your list and reduce campaign spend.

Delivery rate - Monitor this so you can make sure your emails are not ending up in everyones spam box.

Site traffic - Monitor this to determine if email marketing is an effective way to drive quality traffic to your website.

Why A/B Test Every Email You Send

Aim to improve the list of KPIs above and get more sales by A/B testing. It's crucial to get real results. A/B tests allow you to run two versions of an email (or landing page) to see which performs better. This allows you to make improvements faster. For instance, if you start seeing low open rates, that usually means you need to change the subject line or the time of day you are sending the emails.

If you are seeing low click through rates that means your call to actions, graphics or body copy are not correct or enticing enough. Also be sure to make sure your emails are optimized for mobile. 75% of people who engage with your email will probably be opening it on their phone, so make sure it looks right. Don't forget to send a test email to yourself first to check.

You should be A/B Split Testing the Following:

Call to Actions: Such as "Buy Now" vs. "Click Here"

Subject Lines: Personalized vs. non-personalized, specials on specific products vs. categories

To include or not to include testimonials

The Visual Layout of the message: One column vs. two columns

Name Personalization: "Hello Jessica!" vs. "Hey there!"

Text in the Email: Having lots of wordy copy vs. mostly images and pictures

How to End Up in the Inbox and Not Spam

When you send your emails, you need to avoid the SPAM folder. Your promotions won't get noticed or read if it ends up there. Use these simple tips to avoid getting sent to spam.

1. **Don't Buy Lists -** These lists sometimes are filled with fake, dead or emails of people who never gave you consent to email them. They will either mark you as spam or since you are unsolicited you will end up in the SPAM box automatically. This will add a strike against your domain.

2. **Don't Use Spammy Words -** The email providers have really strong SPAM filters nowadays and they have a list of "keywords" that will automatically trigger and mark you as SPAM. Words like "As seen on", "Meet Singles", "Buy Direct", "Earn $", "Money Making Opportunity", "Bargain", "Compare Rates", 'Credit", "Fast Cash", "Incredible Deal", "Miracle", "Get Paid", "Click Below", "Cure" etc.

3. **Certify Your Domain** - If you have a real website with a real domain, quickly verify it with your email marketing provider so they ensure your emails always end up in the inbox.

4. **Whitelist -** After your subscribers get added to your list, send them a follow up email asking them to double opt-in. It's just an extra confirmation step to make sure the potential customer really wants to be subscribed on your list.

Chapter 8: Ways to Automate the Email Marketing Process

Email automation is the most effective way to communicate consistently with your customers because it allows you to send out your messages at specific times. By using automation, you can save time by setting up email workflows to send messages when customers take specific actions.

So you can set up trigger emails or drip content. Trigger emails can include welcome emails, getting started emails, abandoning carts, referring a friend, happy birthday, or any specific action or milestone you set up. Drip emails are a sequence of emails strung together to bring customers through the sales funnel.

Essentially after they sign up for your free report or download your piece of content in exchange for their email address, they get sent into a funnel that sends them useful content or asks for their attention to book an appointment or purchase a recommended product. You can easily set up either type of campaign with your chosen email marketing provider.

STEPS TO AUTOMATION

Step 1 : Choose an FREE offer type: Infographic, Video, Web Course, Free Trial Offer, Product Sample, Event Tickets, Templates, Software App, Podcast, Music, Game, PDF Report, Personal Consultation, Webinar, Membership, Money Back, Newsletter, Catalog, Price List, Coupon / Discount, Product Release Notice, Survey Results.

Step 2: Select the Right Opt-in Email Collection Method : Website Opt-in Form, Lightbox, Shopping Cart, Direct Mail, Video Overlay, Contest Sign Up, Course Signup, Support Form, Software Registration, Event Signup, Account Sign Up, Webinar Signup, Office Visit, Mobile App Download, Phone Call Collection.

Step 3: Choose a campaign type: Drip or Trigger Automation. Engage the new subscribers with a welcome email. Deliver the Promised Value, then send them through a sequence that will up-sell / engage with good design, product benefits, credibility, social proof, a push for urgency, bonus offers.

Once you set this up and choose what emails come after the next in the sequence, anyone who opt's into your funnel will automatically receive messages and offers from you without you having to manually repeat it over and over again.

Chapter 9: Email Marketing Resources

Graphic River - This website has the best email templates to get you started. They are easy to use and edit. They even sell a service that can help you customize the templates.

Here's a List of Useful Templates by style:

Corporate Email Templates

Modern Email Templates

Fashion Email Templates

Real Estate Email Templates

Technology Email Templates

Fitness Email Templates

Fiverr - This website has plenty of freelancers that will help you organize, create and send your emails.

Here's a List of Useful Email Gigs:

Email Marketing - General

Content Writers

Email Funnel

Appendix: "Email Marketing FAQs"

Q: What's the best way to build an email marketing strategy?

A: First, decide on what your email marketing goals are. To make up-sell / cross sell and make money, to build trust, or just to send out general updates / communications on your brand. Next make sure that each part of your email aligns with that goal. The pictures, the text and the call to actions. Lastly create a process for continuous improvement and document each growth and achievement as well as failures.

Q: Should I just buy a list to kick off my marketing efforts?

A: You can, but since your message is unsolicited, there's a big percentage chance your message will end up with a low response rate or in the spam folder. These people in the list never heard of your company or brand and usually never even know where you got their email address from. You will easily be regarded as an intruder.

Q: How do I know if my email campaign was successful?

A: Everyone's measure of success is different. Your first goal should be to shoot for as many opens as possible, second would be clicks through to the website and last actual conversions or sales via this sales channel (email marketing).

Q: How often should I send emails?

A: Send it as often as people want or expect to hear from you. That could be one email a day, every morning, or it could be once a week. I wouldn't recommend anything more than once a day or a few times a week. Too many can start to get annoying and increase unsubscribes

Q: How can segmenting my emails help me?

A: Use this feature to send the right message to the right person at the right time. After you start getting some facts and figures on your reports, you can now tailor your emails to different segments of people.

For instance, you can send emails or offers to people who are just brand new to your list, people who didn't open at all, people who **DID** open, but didn't click or convert, people who are opening and clicking but not buying or converting, or the people who open, clicked and purchased. This would help target your message to the right customer lifecycle stage.

Q: Are there any rules I need to adhere to before sending an email blast?

A: Most email providers will walk you through these steps at the time of setup, however you'll need to include an unsubscribe link, include your brick and mortar address or P.O. box, agree to a statement claiming the list is yours and you didn't purchase it.

Appendix B: Recommended Resources

Email Marketing - Aweber

The world's best email marketing software for content marketing newsletters and auto-responders! Create emails with style and get more messages delivered fast! Create professional and powerful email marketing today.

Get a Free Trial of Aweber for Email Marketing

Web Hosting - Bluehost

I highly recommend using Bluehost for your website. They have an incredibly easy to use 1-click automatic word press installation and amazing customer service. The link below gets you a special discount off the regular price!

Get a 30 Day Money Back Guarantee for a New Website

Business Incorporation - MyCorporation

Everything you need to start, maintain and protect your business. Easily form a corporation or Limited Liability Company in no time. Learn which entity is best for your business!

Legally Incorporate Your Business Today

Appendix B: Recommended Resources

Business Supply Purchases - Amazon Business

Create a free Amazon Business account to save time and money on business purchases with competitive B2B prices and discounts. Satisfy your sourcing requirements and get Tax-exempt purchasing.

[Get Discounted Supplies with Amazon for Business](#)

Email Marketing Designs - 99designs

I've always trusted them with creating online graphics, logos and website designs. You can use them for all sorts of projects like packaging, email marketing designs, banner ads, business cards, trade show material and more.

[Get Email Marketing Designed Today](#)

Credit Card & Payment Processing - Square

Square helps millions of event companies run their business from secure credit card processing to point of sale solutions. Get paid faster with Square. Sign up today!

[Signup for Square for Business](#)

About the Author

MARKETING EXPERT | BRAND STRATEGIST BUSINESS COACH | TV HOST

This Business Coach and Marketing Expert has shared her passion for growing brands from the ground up. She's worked with Startups, Small Businesses, Fortune 500 Corporations and entertainment talent that recognize the value of marketing. She gives her clients the ability to access their niche market via online, social media, mobile, merchandising, and events.

The What's Your Game Plan Show features free expert advice and growth strategies for Business Owners and Executives across the globe.

Access thousands of FREE Tips, Trends and Tools to Move Your Business Forward! Contact the author:

AdellaPasos.com
Subscribe to Business Strategy TV Youtube

www.ingramcontent.com/pod-product-compliance
Lightning Source LLC
Chambersburg PA
CBHW081706220526
45466CB00009B/2898